I0022646

Bernard Tindal Bosanquet

Our Banking System and the Sufficiency or Insufficiency of our Cash Reserves

Bernard Tindal Bosanquet

Our Banking System and the Sufficiency or Insufficiency of our Cash Reserves

ISBN/EAN: 9783743404663

Manufactured in Europe, USA, Canada, Australia, Japa

Cover: Foto ©Suzi / pixelio.de

Manufactured and distributed by brebook publishing software
(www.brebook.com)

Bernard Tindal Bosanquet

Our Banking System and the Sufficiency or Insufficiency of our Cash Reserves

AND

The Sufficiency or Insufficiency

OF

OUR CASH RESERVES.

BY

BERNARD TINDAL BOSANQUET.

LONDON:

EFFINGHAM WILSON & CO., ROYAL EXCHANGE.

1892.

PREFACE.

ALTHOUGH the question of the sufficiency or insufficiency of the cash reserves of the country is one which attracted considerable attention at the beginning of last year, when Mr. Goschen delivered his famous speech at Leeds, very little action has hitherto been taken in the matter; and the present may not be an inopportune time at which to consider whether any further action is required. For nearly two years the country has been labouring under one of those periods of depression which invariably follow any great crisis. There are now some signs of improvement, and of the return of better times; but when the good time comes people very soon forget the lesson of the past. In the following treatise the Author has endeavoured to show that the banks are not altogether to blame for the periodical crises to which our banking system is at present exposed, and has made some attempt to indicate the nature and extent of the remedy. For his statistics he is indebted to Mr. Crump's "Key to the London Market" (which, unfortunately, has only been carried to the close of the year 1876), Mr. Palgrave's "Bank Acts and Bank Rate," Mr. Haupt's "The Monetary Question in 1892," and Mr. Skinner's "London Banks and Kindred Companies and Firms."

CLAYSMORE,
   ENFIELD,
      October 19th, 1892.

OUR BANKING SYSTEM:

AND THE

SUFFICIENCY OR INSUFFICIENCY

OF

OUR CASH RESERVES.

THE banking system of the United Kingdom is a gigantic fabric of credit, built up upon a solid foundation of gold. The deposits held by the banks are not cash, but merely banking credits, although the depositors have the right at any time of demanding payment of them in gold. The term " gold " may be taken to include the notes of the Bank of England and the coined silver and bronze in circulation and in the tills of the banks. The total amount of gold in the country being, probably, not much more than one-fifth of the total of those deposits or banking credits, it is obvious that the right of demanding payment can exist to a limited extent only; because if holders of more than one-fifth of them were to demand payment in gold at the same time, it would be impossible for the banks to meet the demand, even supposing the whole stock of gold in the country to be available for that purpose, which would not

be the case. In a similar manner a club may
have five thousand members, each member having an equal right to the use of the club. Supposing that there were only accommodation for
one thousand, it is obvious that only one-fifth of
the members could make use of the club at the
same time.

Nearly all the larger transactions for which
money is required, whether it be in connection
with trade and commerce, or the receipt and payment of debts by persons in private life, are
effected by transfers of banking credits from
debtor to creditor. Without a banking system
such as exists in this country it would be impossible for the trade of the country to be carried on ;
the immediate effect of a well-established banking
system being to economise, to an enormous
extent, the use of gold. The gold in circulation,
that is to say, the gold in the pockets of the
people, is required for purposes for which banking
credits are not available ; and however highly-
organised and widespread a banking system may
be, a certain amount of gold must always be required for such purposes. Although the estab-
lishment of banks in places where they have not
hitherto existed will, to a great extent, displace
gold, and cause it to return to the centre, it can
never do so altogether. The greater the banking
facilities of a country, the less in proportion to
the population and wealth of that country will be
the amount of gold required for internal circulation.

The reserve of gold—that is to say, the gold in
the tills of the banks, added to the reserve of the

Bank of England—forms the connecting link between cash transactions and banking credits. Apart from any increase or decrease resulting from an excess of the imports of gold over exports, or the reverse; whenever there is an increase in the amount of gold in circulation there must be a corresponding decrease in the reserve; and, similarly, a contraction of the circulation must cause a corresponding increase. The reserve of the country is the gold not actually in circulation; the reserve of the banks, including the Bank of England, the amount held in reserve by the latter. Of these two reserves the former, which includes the latter, has to answer two purposes. It is at the same time the source from which any gap in the circulation is filled up, and the foundation on which the banking system of the country is supported.

At certain periods in the year, notably during the autumn, when a large amount of coin is required for the payment of wages in connection with the crops and harvest, there is a natural expansion of the circulation. The effect of such an expansion is to diminish the reserve, and, probably, at the same time to diminish to some extent the bankers' deposits.

Again, in a time of great commercial prosperity, not only is there more employment for labour, but wages have a tendency to rise, and these two causes bring about a natural demand for gold. The reserve must be depleted to the extent of that demand; but it does not follow that there will be a similar depletion of deposits. On the contrary, the deposits of the banks at such times frequently show a tendency to increase. Concurrently with the demand for gold there arises an additional demand for advances, for trade purposes, and at the same time depositors can afford to keep larger balances with their bankers. The result is an increase in the advances made by bankers, and in the "other securities" of the Bank of England, and the two would together equal the additional amount of gold in circulation added to the increase in the bankers' deposits. The term "other securities" includes bills discounted, loans to brokers, and loans to ordinary customers. Thirdly, an apparent increase in the circulation, and a corresponding depletion of the reserve, may arise through timid depositors, in a time of panic drawing out their deposits in the shape of notes and coin which they do not want, and do not know what to do with. The gold so withdrawn is never really in circulation, but is simply hoarded; and as the panic subsides it invariably finds its way back to the reserve.

In the event of a widespread panic, the London banks are not only called upon to supply gold to their own customers, but the country banks at once take steps to strengthen their reserves by obtaining a further supply of gold through their London agents. The latter, in their turn, must either allow their balances at the Bank of England to run down, or strengthen their balances by calling in money from the brokers. If, as would probably be the case at such a time, none of the banks are lenders, the brokers are driven to the Bank of England for assistance, the final result being an increase in the "other securities" and a corresponding decrease in the reserve, the bankers' balances remaining much as before.

It appears from the above that an expansion of the circulation may arise from two causes : the first being the legitimate demand which arises in prosperous times, and at certain periods of the year ; the second, the fictitious demand which arises in times of panic. When it is certain that the increased demand, though perfectly legitimate, is merely temporary, the reserve may safely be allowed to fall to a comparatively low point ; but when such a demand is the result of great activity in trade, and is not only likely to continue for a lengthened period, but possibly to increase, the case is different.

In the latter case the rates charged for advances are invariably high, being governed by the ordinary laws of supply and demand, and borrowers being able to afford to pay high rates ; and the natural effect of these high rates is to attract capital from other countries, and to add to the supply of gold. By this means the reserve may be kept at a sufficiently high level, without the adoption of any extraordinary methods for replenishing it. In the case of a fictitious demand for gold, arising through want of confidence, the remedy is not so easy to find. A severe panic seldom lasts very long, so that the imposition of a high rate of interest is no remedy, because the panic would probably be over before it would have time to take effect, and it would merely have the effect of intensifying the panic. So long as the panic lasts the reserve grows smaller and smaller, although all the time the supply of gold in the country may be far in excess of all legitimate requirements. A panic is invariably followed by a long period of stagnation, and during such a period the amount of gold in circulation would probably be less than it was before the commencement of the panic. The question is, how far is it necessary or desirable to keep a special store of gold to meet such contingencies, and by whom is the burden of keeping it to be borne?

The great panic which succeeded the failure of Overend, Gurney, & Co. commenced on May 11th, 1866, and the return of the Bank of England for the week ending May 16th showed that the reserve had declined during that week from £4,950,325 to £730,830. During the week ending May 2nd there had been a decline of about £1,000,000 in the reserve, but the following week showed an increase of about £110,000. The week ending May 23rd showed an increase, as compared with that ending May 16th, of about £100,000, the reserve then being £830,865; but during the following week there was a further decline to £415,410, the lowest amount ever shown in the published returns.

The Bank Charter Act was then suspended, and the Bank authorised to make a further issue of fiduciary notes to the extent of £5,000,000. At the same time it was stipulated that the rate of interest should be raised to 10 per cent. This at once allayed the panic; it was not found necessary to make use of the further authorised issue of fiduciary notes, and on June 6th the reserve had increased to £2,167,405. On June

27th it had increased to £4,346,545, after which
date it again gradually declined, until on August 1st
it was reduced to £2,412,390. From that date
there was a steady and almost uninterrupted
increase up to the end of the year ; and on
December 26th the amount of the reserve was
£11,374,515.

On August 22nd the Bank of England reduced
its rate to eight per cent., and a further reduction
of one per cent. was made in each of the three
following weeks ; and on December 26th the rate
was reduced to three and a half per cent. On
July 31st, 1867, it was reduced to two per cent.,
and remained at that point until November 25th,
1868. Between April 25th and May 30th, 1866,
the " other securities" increased from £18,507,854
to £33,447,463, an increase of £14,939,609 ; and
the " Government Securities " from £10,694,254
to £10,864,638, an increase of £170,384 ; making
a total increase from these two sources of
£15,109,993. During the same period the reserve
of notes was reduced from £5,844,205 to £415,410,
a reduction of £5,428,795 ; and the gold and
silver in the banking department of the Bank of
England was reduced to the extent of £405,886 ;
making a total reduction in the reserve of
£5,834,681. The net result of the above figures
was an increase of £9,275,612 on the side of
assets. On the other side of the account the
" public deposits " increased from £4,417,147 to
£6,188,512, an increase of £1,771,365; and the
" other deposits," which include the bankers'
balances, from £13,294,641 to £20,467,080, an
increase of £7,172,439 ; being a total increase of

£8,943,804. The difference of £331,808 between
the totals of the two above sets of figures was
counterbalanced by an increase in the "rest"
or undivided profits of the Bank of England, and
in the "seven-day and other bills," amounting in
the aggregate to the same figure.

The bankers' balances during the same period
increased from £5,062,000 to £7,881,000, an
increase of £2,819,000; leaving an increase in
the "other deposits" from other sources of
£4,353,439. This large increase was to some
extent due to the brokers and merchants having
obtained large advances from the Bank, in order
not only to meet the present demands upon them,
but also to strengthen their resources in order to
meet any further possible demands; and it was
also in a great measure due to the new accounts
opened by the public.

It has been said that the Bank of England, at
that time, opened 700 new accounts in one week.
On June 20th the increase in the other deposits
since April 25th amounted to £5,062,357; but by
the end of the year it had declined to £3,731,224.
Between April 25th and May 30th the coin and
bullion in both departments of the Bank declined
from £13,855,776 to £11,878,775, being a decrease
of £1,977,001. It is probable that this decrease
was entirely due to the additional amount of coin
in circulation, or hoarded; but without statistics
it is impossible to say whether it was not in some
degree due to withdrawals of gold for export. It
is more probable, however, that the imports of gold
at that time exceeded the exports, in which case
the absorption of coin for circulation, &c., was

greater than the decrease in the coin and bullion in the vaults of the Bank.

So far as the notes in the Issue Department of the Bank are concerned, a withdrawal of coin has precisely the same effect whether it be withdrawn for export or for internal circulation. When coin is withdrawn in exchange for notes, there would be a reduction to the extent of the withdrawal in the amount of the notes issued and of the notes in circulation, but the reserve would remain unaltered. When coin is withdrawn in exchange for a draft on the Bank, there would be a reduction to the extent of the withdrawal in the amount of the notes issued and of the reserve, but the amount of the notes in circulation would remain unaltered. Supposing the amount of the notes issued to be £40,000,000, the amount of those in circulation £24,000,000 and the amount of the reserve £16,000,000, and notes to the extent of £5,000,000 to be presented for payment in gold ; the whole of that gold might be exported the next day, but the reserve would still amount to £16,000,000, while the amount of the notes issued and the notes in circulation would be reduced respectively to £35,000,000 and £19,000,000. It follows from this that the amount of the reserve is not a reliable index of the sufficiency or in-sufficiency of the stock of gold. The reserve may apparently be high, because the amount of coin in circulation is below the average, owing to slackness of trade or other causes ; and in that case if gold is allowed to drift away, as soon as there arises a revival of trade and an increase in the amount of gold required for circulation, it may be found that the reserve has been allowed to fall to a point sufficiently low to create uneasiness and alarm.

In the absence of any reliable statistics as to the total amount of gold in the country and the amount in actual circulation, it is difficult to estimate the amount required to constitute a safe and sufficient reserve. According to Mr. Haupt's estimate, the entire stock of gold in the country at the beginning of the current year was £118,000,000, of which £103,000,000 was composed of sovereigns and half-sovereigns. Sir Charles Fremantle estimated the amount of coined gold at the end of the year 1890 at £105,000,000, which Mr. Martin and Mr. Palgrave have estimated it as not exceeding £69,000,000 ; but this latter estimate is probably considerably too low. Supposing the entire stock of gold, coined and uncoined, at the end of last year to have been about £100,000,000 ; adding to this amount £16,450,000 the amount of the fiduciary issue of notes, £26,000,000 the estimated amount of coined silver in circulation and in the tills of the banks, and £1,900,000 the estimated amount of bronze coin, the entire stock of gold, or its equivalent, at that time would have been, say, £145,000,000. The reserve of the Bank of England on December 30th, 1891, stood at rather more than £13,000,000, leaving £132,000,000 as the amount in circulation and in the tills of the banks. The question now arises, how much of this latter amount was in circulation, that is to say, in the pockets of the people, and how much was held by the banks ?

On December 31st, 1891, the liabilities of the twenty-four banks, which were at that time members of the Clearing House, amounted to £253,000,000, and their cash in hand and at the Bank of England to upwards of £35,000,000. There were at the same time seventeen other banks, including the Scotch banks, with offices in London, whose published accounts showed liabilities to the extent of about £127,000,000, and cash in hand and at the Bank of England to the extent of nearly £13,000,000. These latter figures, added to those of the clearing banks, make a total of liabilities £380,000,000, and cash, &c., £48,000,000. Supposing the liabilities of the remaining banks throughout the United Kingdom to have been £300,000,000, and their cash, &c., £20,000,000, the gross totals for all the banks would be: liabilities £680,000,000, and cash in hand and at Bank of England £68,000,000. Assuming the amount of the bankers' balances to have been £12,000,000, the amount in the tills of the banks would have been £56,000,000, and the distribution of the entire stock of gold as follows :—

Reserve of the Bank of England	...	£18,000,000
Notes and coin in the tills of banks	...	56,000,000
,, ,, circulation	... ...	76,000,000
		£145,000,000

As the amount of gold in circulation increases, the reserve has a tendency to decrease; but it does not follow that an increase in the circulation to the extent of, say, £5,000,000, would involve a corresponding decrease in the reserve; because, under ordinary circumstances, the banks might regard the expansion as only temporary, and allow the gold in their tills to run down to some extent.

If the above estimates are fairly accurate, it is probable that the amount of gold in circulation varies between £70,000,000 as a minimum, and £85,000,000 as an extreme maximum.

During the panic of 1866, when the increase in the circulation was purely fictitious, the expansion at no time exceeded £8,000,000. It is inconceivable that any legitimate demand for gold for currency purposes could absorb even one-fourth of the reserve of the country, that is to say, the reserve of gold at the Bank of England and in the tills of the banks. On the basis of the above figures, supposing the average amount of gold in circulation to be as much as £80,000,000, the absorption of one-fourth of the reserve would involve an increase in the circulation of upwards of £16,000,000, being more than double the increase which took place during the panic of 1866. Even supposing that so large an increase in the circulation were to take place, there would still be a reserve of nearly £50,000,000. If so large a margin of reserve is insufficient to prevent periodical panics, it is difficult to form any idea as to how large an addition to the reserve, short of bringing it to the point at which it would equal the liabilities, would suffice to prevent them.

If the reserve of the country is ample to meet any legitimate expansion of the circulation, it is at least open to argument whether a temporary suspension of the Bank Act is not the true remedy for a crisis brought about by the unreasoning folly of panic-stricken depositors. It must be the ultimate remedy when all other means have failed. Such an operation as the borrowing of gold from the Bank of France may be effective, but it is not a source of supply which can be or ought to be relied upon. In times of panic it is not the men of business who make a rush to convert their balances with their bankers into gold; on the contrary, they would more probably take steps to increase their balances, in order to be in a better position to meet any losses or exceptional demands. A man of business might, if he had lost confidence in his banker, transfer his account to some other bank; but this would be merely a transfer of banking credits, and would in no way affect the reserve.

The depositors who create or intensify a panic are of a very different class. They consist for the most part of those to whom it is not an absolute necessity to keep any considerable sum in hand, and who, as soon as they hear that there is any pressure for money, think it advisable, for their own protection, to convert their balances into cash. If the number of the depositors who adopt that course is very great, the result is a a struggle for who is to be the first to get his money; as was the case in the recent very foolish run on the Birkbeck Bank. In all probability, at least nine-tenths of this class of depositors would see no danger in an unlimited issue of fiduciary paper, provided it was authorised by the British Government; and the mere fact of a further issue being authorised, as was actually the case in 1866, would suffice to allay their fears. Although a comparatively small addition to the reserve may suffice to allay a panic, it would require a very large addition to the stock of gold to render a panic practically impossible.

A reduction in the reserve arising from an excess of the exports of gold over the imports involves far more danger than a reduction arising from an expansion of the circulation ; and the long continuance of a drain of gold might give rise to well-founded alarm.. In such a case the only remedy is to raise the rate of interest, and to continue to raise it until it suffices not only to stop the drain, but to bring back the gold which has been allowed to leave the country. This is a remedy which has always hitherto been found effectual, and which will continue to be effectual so long as the credit of the country is maintained at its present high level. The application of it is one of the duties which devolves on the Bank of England, as the bank of issue and the custodian of the reserve ; but it is the duty of the other banks, and it is for their own interests to give all support to the Bank of England in any such emergency.

It has been said that the banks do not give sufficient support to the Bank of England, and that when a crisis supervenes the whole burden of meeting the crisis is thrown upon that institution ; and it has been further alleged that this is one reason why the country is exposed to the risk of periodical panics. In other words, the banks are accused of employing their resources too nearly up to the hilt, and not keeping sufficiently large balances with the Bank of England.

Whether or not this is a just charge, it is an absolute fact that if the banks, by curtailing their advances, were to increase their balances at the Bank, they would not add one iota to the reserve. The amount of the reserve is simply the difference between the entire stock of gold in the country and the amount in circulation and in the tills of the banks, so that the only possibly way in which the banks could add to the reserve would be by reducing the amount of gold in their tills. Instead of saying that the Bank of England keeps the reserve, it would be more correct to say that the reserve keeps itself at the Bank of England. The Bank cannot, by any direct action of its own, add to or diminish the amount of the reserve. It does not follow that an increase in the advances made by the Bank would have any effect on the reserve. For instance, supposing the advances to be increased to the extent of £5,000,000, unless gold were required for circulation or export, the persons to whom the advances were made would draw cheques on the Bank which would be presented for payment through the other banks ; the final result being an increase in the bankers' balances to the extent of the advances. As far as the Bank of England is concerned, the result would be precisely the same as if the other banks had called in £5,000,000 of their advances, and increased their balances to the same extent, and the Bank had re-lent the money.

Before proceeding further, it may be useful to form an estimate of the average amount of the liabilities and the reserve of the Bank of England and of the bankers' balances. In forming that

estimate. it will be more convenient to confine the
term "other banks" to those banks which are
members of the Clearing House, and whose balances comprise the bulk of the bankers' balances.
The highest point ever reached by the reserve was
shown in the return for the week ending September
20th, 1876, when it amounted to £21,432,515,
exclusive of the gold and silver coin in the banking department. The average amount for the
year, exclusive of gold, was rather over £14,000,000;
and supposing the gold and silver coin to have
averaged £1,000,000, the total average of the
reserve for 1876 was about £15,000,000. The
average amount for the period 1885–91 was
£13,702,000. During the fifty-two weeks com-
mencing with the week ending September 23rd,
1891, and ending with the week ending September
14th, 1892, the highest point reached by the
reserve was £18,278,124 on June 22nd, 1892, and
the lowest point touched was £12,599,556 on
November 4th, 1891, the average being about
£15,700,000. During that period it is probable
that the amount of the reserve was rather above
than below the average, so that, judging by the
above figures, £15,000,000 may be considered a
fair estimate of the average amount. The total
liabilities of the Bank during the same period
averaged about £36,500,000. The average amounts
for the forty-seven previous years were as under :—

1845–54	....	....	£17,730,000
1855–64	....	....	19,810,000
1865–74	....	....	25,690,000
1875–84	....	....	30,880,000
1885 –91		....	32,630,000

The present average may be taken to be £35,000,000, making the average proportion of reserve to liabilities nearly 43 per cent. With regard to the bankers' balances there are no statistics to hand subsequent to the end of the year 1875. In 1857 their average amount was rather over £3,000,000; in 1861 it had increased to upwards of £4,000,000; in 1866 to about £7,000,00; and in 1871 to upwards of £8,000,000. In 1875 they were at their maximum on July 28th, when they amounted to £14,572,000, and the lowest point touched was £7,072,000 on May 5th, the average for the year being about £10,500,000. During the last seventeen years there has been an enormous increase in the liabilities of the banks, and a considerable increase during the last two years in the proportion of their cash in hand and at the Bank of England to their liabilities; so that at the present time it is probable that £12,000,000 would not be an over-estimate of the average amount of the bankers' balances. At the close of the year 1888 there were twenty-five banks which were members of the Clearing House, but of these only sixteen published their balance-sheets. The accounts of these latter, made up to the 31st December in that year, showed liabilities £173,000,000, and cash in hand and at the Bank of England £21,667,000; the proportion of cash to liabilities being about 12½ per cent. On December 31st, 1890, the liabilities of these sixteen banks had risen to about £202,000,000, their cash in hand, &c., to about £26,500,000, and the proportion of cash to liabilities to 13·1 per cent. At the end of last

year the number of banks which were members of
the Clearing House was twenty-four ; the amount
of their liabilities was £253,000,000 ; of their
cash in hand, &c., £35,360,000 ; and the proportion of cash to liabilities 13·9 per cent.

Although the bankers' balances are a very large
source of profit to the Bank of England, they
constitute an element rather of weakness than of
strength as far as the Bank itself is concerned.
The larger their balances the greater is the parti-
cipation of the banks in the final reserve, and
they are entitled at any moment to withdraw the
whole amount. Taking the above estimates as
a basis—namely, reserve £15,000,000, liabilities
£35,000,000, bankers' balances £12,000,000, and
proportion of reserve to liabilities 43 per cent. : of
the £15,000,000 which constitutes the reserve
only £3,000,000 would really belong to the Bank,
the remaining £12,000,000 being the reserve of
the other banks ; so that, exclusive of the bankers'
balances, the liabilities of the Bank would be
£23,000,000, the reserve £3,000,000, and the
proportion of reserve to liabilities 13 per cent.
If the banks were to increase their balances to the
extent of, say, £5,000,000, by calling in money
from the brokers, and the Bank of England
increased its advances to brokers to the same
extent, the position of the Bank would be—reserve
£15,000,000, liabilities £40,000,000, and bankers'
balances £17,000,000. The proportion of reserve
to liabilities would still be as much as 37½ per
cent., and it would be said that the Bank of
England was keeping 37½ per cent. of its liabilities
in reserve, against only 16 per cent. on the part of

the other banks. The very next day the banks
might withdraw the whole of their balances in
notes and coin, in which case the reserve of the
Bank of England would not only be exhausted,
but would be insufficient to the extent of £2,000,000
to meet the demand. Again, supposing it to be
deemed advisable to increase the stock of gold in
the country by, say, £10,000,000, and the "other
banks" undertook to bear the whole burden and
expense of that increase ; the figures of the Bank
of England would then be—reserve £25,000,000,
liabilities £45,000,000, and bankers' balances
£22,000,000. The Bank of England would then
claim to be keeping $55\frac{1}{2}$ per cent. of its liabilities
in reserve, against 18 per cent. on the part of the
other banks. The Bank might then employ the
whole of the £10,000,000 thus added to its
resources, and allow gold to the same amount
(being the gold imported at the expense of the
other banks) to be taken for export, and still claim
to be keeping one-third of its liabilities in reserve,
against only 18 per cent. on the part of the other
banks.

In support of the theory that the Bank of
England is entitled to include the bankers'
balances as part of its own reserve, it is argued
that the Bank is entitled to deal with them in the
same manner as it deals with the deposits of
ordinary customers. It is held, in fact, that the
two are exactly analogous, and that the Bank of
England cannot be expected to take the trouble
and assume the responsibility of keeping the
bankers' balances unless it is in a position to
make some profit out of them. If the bankers'

balances were really analogous to the ordinary deposits, there would be some reason in such a contention, but they are not. They constitute the cash reserve of the banks over and above the the cash in their tills, and every banker regards his balance at the Bank as being equivalent to cash in his till. As far as the trouble of keeping their balances is concerned, an average balance of £2,000 kept by each clearing bank, or, say, £50,000 in all, would be more than ample compensation. With regard to the responsibility, the mere existence of these balances is a full and sufficient remuneration. Supposing, as above, the reserve to be £15,000,000, the liabilities £35,000,000, and the bankers' balances £12,000,000; if the bankers withdrew their balances, the reserve would be reduced to £3,000,000, and the liabilities to £23,000,000; and the Bank of England in order to keep up the average proportion of 43 per cent. of reserve to liabilities, would be compelled to add about £6,900,000 to its reserve. Supposing the average rate at which the Bank of England can employ its resources to be three per cent., the above addition to the reserve would involve a loss to the Bank of upwards of £200,000 a year. It may be said, therefore, that the bankers' balances are worth £200,000 a year to the Bank supposing them to be kept entirely unemployed. As a matter of fact, the Bank employs on average about 57 per cent. of these balances, or about £6,840,000. The interest on that amount, at three per cent., would be rather more than £205,000 a year; so that altogether the bankers' balances may be said to be worth upwards of £400,000 a year to the Bank of England, or more than one-fourth of the entire profits. In the face of this it is said that the banks do not give sufficient support to the Bank of England, and ought to keep larger balances. If they increase their balances to any considerable extent, the amount to which they would be entitled to participate in the reserve would considerably exceed the actual amount of the reserve. When the amount of the bankers' balances is in excess of the amount of the reserve, not only is the Bank of England keeping no reserve, but the bankers are allowing the Bank to employ a portion of their money over and above their balances for its own benefit.

It has further been held that only a portion of the bankers' balances can be regarded as cash, because a considerable portion is required for the purpose of carrying out the daily settlement at the Clearing House. This, again, is an erroneous contention, because, although it may be a convenience to the banks to make use of their balances for such a purpose, there is no absolute necessity to employ cash, or its equivalent, in order to effect mere transfers of banking credits from one bank to another. Whereas it is the existence of the bankers' balances which has led to their being employed for such a purpose ; it is assumed that this secondary purpose, for which they are to some extent employed, has led to their existence. Although the aggregate liabilities of the banks do not as a rule vary to any great extent from day to day, there may frequently be a considerable variation in the liabilities of individual banks. For instance, when the railway companies pay their dividends, there would be a considerable decrease in the liabilities of the banks holding large railway deposits. On the other hand, the liabilities of the other banks would show a corresponding increase, because the dividend warrants are invariably crossed, and are, with some few trifling exceptions, presented for payment through the Clearing House. Such operations are merely transfers of banking credits. Under the present system, the banks which hold large railway deposits call in money, while the remaining banks lend a similar amount, and there is little variation in the aggregate amount of the deposits and of the money lent at call.

Supposing that on a given day each of the clearing banks transferred to a central fund at the Clearing House a certain portion of its money lent at call, in accordance with a scale previously arranged, and the aggregate amount so transferred were £12,000,000, the banks would still have upwards of £20,000,000 lent at call over and above the amount so transferred. If the call money transferred to the Clearing House were employed, as the bankers' balances are at present employed, for carrying out the daily settlement, at the end of each day some banks would have less call money at the Clearing House than they had at the end of the previous settlement, and some more, but the aggregate amount would always be £12,000,000. If any banker wished to increase the amount of his call money at the Clearing House, he could do so by calling in from the brokers a sum sufficient to render him a creditor at the daily settlement to the required extent. Similarly, he would reduce the amount of his call money at the Clearing House by lending money to the brokers, and thus rendering himself a debtor. One advantage of such a system would be, that a banker would never have any large unemployed balances at the end of the day, because any large sums paid in late in the day, when it might be too late to lend them, would add so much to his call money at the Clearing House, and the money would lend itself. On the other hand, if cheques for a large amount came in unexpectedly for payment late in the day, the effect would be to reduce the amount of his call money at the Clearing House, and would be equivalent to his having called in money to meet the demand.

The same object might be attained by each bank depositing Government securities in lieu of money lent at call; but one objection to such a method would be that whereas the amount of a banker's call money varies from day to day, the amount of his investments only varies when he thinks it advisable to buy or sell stock. A still simpler method would be to keep a ledger at the Clearing House, in which each bank would figure from day to day either as a creditor or debtor. Under such a system it would be easy to make it a disadvantage for any bank to become too large a creditor or debtor; but it might be necessary for each bank to deposit a certain amount of security, because otherwise, in the event of its being known or suspected that any bank was in a weak position it would create a very natural feeling of uneasiness amongst the other banks if that bank were to become a heavy debtor at the Clearing House. The above are mere suggestions, and no attempt has been made to go minutely into details, their main object being to show that the bankers' balances are not indispensable to the Clearing House settlement. If it is not absolutely necessary to keep any portion of them in hand for that purpose, they are an absolute cash reserve over and above the gold in the tills of the banks; and the utmost extent to which they can be increased, and at the same time be a cash reserve to the full extent of their amount, is the difference between their amount for the time being and the reserve of the Bank of England. When their amount is the same as that of the reserve, the whole reserve of the country is in the hands of the banks; and in the event of a demand arising for gold, whether for export or circulation, the Bank of England makes use of the cash reserve of the other banks in order to meet that demand.

It is not intended to suggest that the banks should keep no balances with the Bank of England or even that they should reduce their present average amount; but so long as they are kept as at present, as a supplement to the till-money, the support and strength which they give to the Bank should be fairly acknowledged. So long as they exist it is probable that they will, as a matter of convenience and not of necessity, be made use of in connection with the settlement at the Clearing House.

If the reserve is insufficient for safety, and it be decided to increase the stock of gold in the

country, the banks will, no doubt, be found ready
and willing to bear their fair share of the additional burden and expense entailed by that
increase. Whether or not such an increase is
necessary is another question. As far as the
circulation is concerned, the existing stock of gold
is more than sufficient to meet any conceivable
demand that can arise; as far as the banking
system is concerned, it is impossible to say how
large an increase would suffice to meet any possible demand which might be engendered by a panic.
One of the main causes of panic is, that at the
very time when disquieting rumours are afloat
and there are symptoms of a crisis, the reserve
has been allowed to fall to too low a point; pro-
tective measures are adopted when it is too late,
and merely serve to precipitate the crisis. At the
present time the reserve of the Bank of England
is comparatively high, but the amount of gold in
circulation is probably below the average. During
the last few weeks a considerable quantity of gold
has left the country by driblets; the tendency of
the foreign exchanges is against us, and a drain
has set in which has already had an appreciable
effect on the reserve. Gold is being allowed to
drift away at the very time when there is an
opportunity of strengthening the reserve, or at
least keeping it up to its present level, without
having resort to any extreme measures.*

There are already symptoms of a revival in
trade and of a consequent demand for more gold,
and that demand might very soon reduce the
reserve to a point which would necessitate a
considerable advance in the rate of interest for

* On going to press the Bank Rate has been raised to three per cent.

advances, and so place a check on the revival. When the amount of gold in circulation is below the average, the reserve ought to be kept to at least the same extent above the average ; in other words, the stock of gold should always be kept up to the point at which it will be sufficient, whatever the existing state of circulation may be, to ensure the maintenance of an adequate reserve when the circulation is at its highest, without the necessity of importing gold. Assuming that £15,000,000 would be an adequate reserve when the circulation is at its maximum, and the circulation to vary between £75,000,000 and £85,000,000, a range of £10,000,000 ; when the circulation is at its minimum the amount of the reserve would be £25,000,000. The reserve would then be abnormally high, and there would, apparently, be more gold in the country than was really required. If other countries wanted gold, and the exchanges were against us, there would be a strong temptation to allow a certain amount of gold to be exported; and when more gold was required for circulation, it might be found necessary to take steps for bringing back the gold which had been allowed to leave the country. This apparent plethora of gold would not occur if some scheme could be devised under which the reserve would always remain at about the same level, say, £15,000,000, whether the amount in circulation were high or low.

One method of effecting this would be to let the amount of the fiduciary issue of notes vary directly with the amount of gold in circulation. For instance, supposing the circulation to be at its minimum, let the fiduciary issue of notes be limited to £6,450,000, and the stock of gold increased, if necessary, until the reserve amounts to £15,000,000. For every £1,000,000 of gold absorbed as the circulation increases, let there be a further fiduciary issue to a similar extent. In this manner, when the circulation reached its maximum, the fiduciary issue would also be at its maximum, namely, £16,450,000, and the reserve would still amount to £15,000,000. To carry the above scheme into effect might involve an addition of about £7,000,000 to our stock of gold, and so large an addition could only be made gradually. Although the maintenance of a reserve as suggested might not be an absolute safeguard against panics, it would at least be a considerable step towards their prevention. To render panics virtually impossible would require a very much larger addition to our stock of gold, and the remedy might prove worse than the disease. It is no advantage to a country to have too much gold, but rather the reverse; because gold is unproductive.

It appears to be assumed that if our stock of gold is to be increased to any considerable extent, the whole burden and expense of that increase should be borne by the banks. If the gold already in the country is sufficient to meet all reasonable demands, the banks are already doing all that can reasonably be expected of them. If it be deemed necessary, for the benefit and protection of the whole community, to keep a special store of gold as a reserve against exceptional contingencies, it is not altogether reason-

able that the whole burden of keeping that
exceptional reserve should be borne by a comparatively small section of the community—
namely, the private bankers and the holders of
shares in joint-stock banks. Our banking system
is quite as much a benefit to the country as to
the banks, and the question of the maintenance
of that system on a sufficiently broad and solid
foundation is one that concerns every member of
the United Kingdom.

With regard to the future, the extent to which
our stock of gold can be increased is limited, while
there is no absolute limit to the possible increase of
banking credits. During the decade ending 1890
the estimated increase in the deposits of all the
banks in the United Kingdom was £130,000,000,
being at the rate of about 25 per cent. for the whole
period. Supposing the deposits at the present
time to amount, in round figures, to £700,000,000 ;
if the same ratio of increase were maintained for
the next twenty years, they would then have increased to nearly £1,100,000,000. During the last
decade the ratio of increase of the population was
about $7\frac{1}{2}$ per cent., or less than one-third of the
ratio of increase of the banking deposits. The
effect of the extension of a banking system being
to economise gold, if the percentage of that
extension is greater than the ratio of increase of
population, the ratio of increase of circulation
would probably be less than that of the population. Supposing the ratio of increase of the
circulation to be 5 per cent. in ten years, and
the present average amount of gold in circulation
£80,000,000 ; by the end of the next twenty years

the amount in circulation will have increased to
rather more than £88,000,000. According to the
estimates on page 15, the amount of gold at
present held by all the banks, including their
balances at the Bank of England, is equal to one-
tenth of their liabilities, while the amount in
their tills is equal to about seven-tenths of the
average amount in circulation.

Supposing these proportions to be maintained,
and the liabilities and amount of gold in circulation
twenty years hence to be in accordance with the
above estimates, the banks in the year 1912 will
require about £62,000,000 for till money, while
their total stock of gold will be £110,000,000.
This would make the amount of their balances
at the Bank of England £48,000,000. If they
increased their balances at the Bank in proportion
to the increase in the circulation, their balances
would amount at the end of twenty years to
about £13,230,000. If they increased them in
proportion to the increase in their liabilities, the
amount would be £18,750,000. In the first case,
the total stock of gold in the country would be
£198,000,000 ; in the second, £163,000,000 ; and
in the third, £169,000,000. To these figures any
excess of the reserve of the Bank of England over
the bankers' balances would have to be added.
If the maintenance of a minimum reserve of
£15,000,000 be deemed a sufficient precaution at
the present time, a minimum of about £19,000,000
ought to be sufficient, supposing the liabilities of
the banks to have increased to the point above
indicated. If that be the case, it follows that if
the ratio of increase of liabilities of the banks

exceeds that of the circulation, the proportion of their reserve to their liabilities must have a tendency to decrease.

In conclusion, it may be said that, although the reserve of the country is very far short of the amount which would suffice to be an absolute safeguard against panics, it is neither necessary nor expedient to increase the reserve to any such extent. At the same time there can be little doubt that a moderate increase in the reserve, say an increase of from five to seven millions, is very desirable; and such an increase might be effected gradually without creating any undue pressure. The larger question of keeping a special reserve of gold to meet unforeseen emergencies is one which concerns the whole nation rather than the banks alone.

EFFINGHAM WILSON & Co.. Printers, Royal Exchange, E.C.

www.ingramcontent.com/pod-product-compliance
Lightning Source LLC
Chambersburg PA
CBHW021550270326

41930CB00008B/1455